DOGGY DEFENDERS

NATIONAL GEOGRAPHIC KiDS

CADI
★ ★ ★
THE **FARM** DOG

Lisa M. Gerry
Photographs by Lori Epstein

NATIONAL GEOGRAPHIC
WASHINGTON, D.C.

Meet CADI!

Cadi

Cadi is a **border collie**. She lives on a farm with her family, the Bakers.

Everyone on the farm
has a job to do ...

... including Cadi!

Cadi is a **farm dog.**

Her job is to help take care of the cows!

Every morning, Cadi herds
the cows down the long trail from
their barn to the pasture.
She runs behind them so they
know to walk forward.

Cadi makes sure
no cows get lost.

If a cow starts wandering away,
Cadi **zooms** to one side ...

**and then she *zooms*
to the other side ...**

... until they're all close together again.

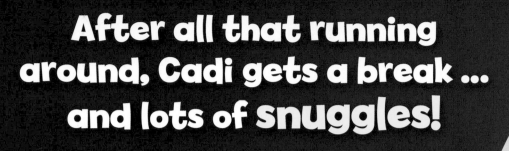

After all that running around, Cadi gets a break ... and lots of **snuggles!**

Now it's time for Cadi's favorite treat: fresh milk! Yum!

Back to work! Cadi visits some more animal friends on the farm.

There are busy turkeys.
Gobble! Gobble!

And smiling goats.
Baa! Baa!

**There are big
muddy pigs.
*Oink! Oink!***

**And noisy
waddling ducks.
*Quack! Quack!***

There are friendly chickens.
Cluck! Cluck!

And there are even little
baby bunnies! *Aww!*

The Baker family loves all their animals, big and small.

Cadi helps keep all of these farm animals **safe.**

Thanks to her, the Baker family can collect tasty eggs and lots of milk.

Sometimes Cadi even helps her family keep an eye on the **vegetable garden!** They pick lots of yummy vegetables to eat for dinner.

But all her hard work has made Cadi **muddy**. Oh no, she has to take a **bath!**

Soon, it will be nighttime.

It's time for the cows to head to the barn, where they will sleep for the night. Cadi gets a ride back to the pasture.

Sniff, sniff!

Even the cows can tell
Cadi had a bath!

Cadi is ready to bring them home.

Cadi **zooms** to one side ...

... then she **zooms** to the other.

She leads all of the cows safely back to the barn.

It has been
a long, happy
day on the farm.
Cadi kept all the
cows safe. Good
job, Cadi!

Meet the Family!

Jessie Baker answers questions about Cadi and working on a farm.

Q How did you get Cadi?

A Years ago, we had sheep on the farm, and we were having trouble moving them from one pasture to another. We heard about a woman whose border collies had just had a litter of puppies. We had seven puppies to choose from. We sat and played with them for two hours! You can't tell if a dog will be a good working dog when it's just a puppy, so we decided to pick one that we fell in love with, and we fell in love with Cadi.

Q **What is Cadi's favorite game to play?**

A Cadi loves to snuggle with us and sometimes play with our other dog, Cuddles. But Cadi's *favorite* thing to do is help and work.

Q **What is the best part of owning a farm dog?**

A It would be nearly impossible to do what we do without Cadi. There is no human who could replace what Cadi does. The animals respect her in a different way than they do us, and she is totally invaluable.

Q **Who trained Cadi?**

A My son Tommy, who was about 10 years old when he started training her.

Q **What do you and Cadi do in your free time?**

A Cadi has a special room in the barn where she relaxes when she's off duty. She loves working so much—we actually have to tell her not to work!

Cadi's Animal Care Tips

Cadi works hard to help take care of the animals at Day Spring Farm. Here are some ways you can be an amazing friend to animals, too.

1. Every animal is different and needs different kinds of care. Learn all you can about the particular kind of animal you're taking care of.

2. Make sure to give the animal plenty of water and feed them only the most healthy foods.

3. Animals, just like humans, need to move their bodies to stay healthy and happy. Make sure the animal you're taking care of gets lots of time to exercise and play.

4. Be sure that your animal has a safe, clean, and comfortable place to live, play, and sleep.

5. Be sure to brush them, bathe them, care for their teeth (if they have any!), and give them lots of love and attention.

6. Don't litter. If trash isn't thrown away in the proper place, it can wind up where it's not supposed to be. Animals might get tangled up in it or think it's food and eat it.

7. Never touch or try to catch an animal that isn't yours. If the animal is wild, let them be, and if they belong to someone else, ask the owner if it's OK to pet them.

8. If you see an animal that has been injured or is in trouble, tell an adult so they can call for help.

386 4586

Since 1888, the National Geographic Society has
funded more than 12,000 research, exploration, and
preservation projects around the world. The Society
receives funds from National Geographic Partners,
LLC, funded in part by your purchase. A portion of
the proceeds from this book supports this vital work.
To learn more, visit natgeo.com/info.

NATIONAL GEOGRAPHIC and Yellow Border Design
are trademarks of the National Geographic Society,
used under license.

For more information, visit nationalgeographic.com,
call 1-877-873-6846, or write to the following address:

National Geographic Partners
1145 17th Street N.W.
Washington, D.C. 20036-4688 U.S.A.

Visit us online at nationalgeographic.com/books

For librarians and teachers: nationalgeographic.com
/books/librarians-and-educators

More for kids from National Geographic: natgeokids.com

National Geographic Kids magazine inspires children to
explore their world with fun yet educational articles on
animals, science, nature, and more. Using fresh story-
telling and amazing photography, Nat Geo Kids shows
kids ages 6 to 14 the fascinating truth about the world—
and why they should care.
kids.nationalgeographic.com/subscribe

For rights or permissions inquiries, please contact
National Geographic Books Subsidiary Rights:
bookrights@natgeo.com

Designed by Callie Broaddus

The publisher would like to thank Lisa M. Gerry, author;
Lori Epstein, photographer; Paige Towler, project editor and series creator; Shannon Hibberd, photo editor;
Shannon Pallatta, graphic designer; Molly Reid, production editor; Anne LeongSon and Gus Tello, production
assistants; and Cadi, the Baker family, and everyone on
the Day Spring Farm.

Hardcover ISBN: 978-1-4263-3679-9
Reinforced library binding ISBN: 978-1-4263-3680-5

Printed in Hong Kong
20/PPHK/1